Front Porch Perspectives

Observations of Nature and the Nature of Life

Volume I

Kathryn Gerwig

Previous publications by Kathryn Gerwig

Calming Your Canine
"One Simple Step to a Better Behaved Pet"

Front Porch Perspectives

Observations of Nature and the Nature of Life

Volume I

Kathryn Gerwig

Penny Mason Publications

~ Words of wisdom and mystery, wit and whimsy ~

pennymasonpublications.com

Front Porch Perspectives

Observations of Nature and the Nature of Life

Volume I

Kathryn Gerwig

ISBN-9781979534130

Printed by Create Space, an Amazon Company

Penny Mason Publications
~ Words of wisdom and mystery, wit and whimsy
~pennymasonpublications.com

Introduction

Works of authors who are keen observers of wildlife and weather have sustained me through me through stressful times. Lessons for living can be found in the reassuring rhythms of the seasons.

I share this collection of comments and essays in the hope of enriching the lives of others who appreciate the inspiration provided by nature. This volume includes summer and early autumn experiences most of which were recorded in a year when I was recovering from injuries incurred in an accident, the healing process aided by days spent outside my door, once I had reached the point when that was possible.

Entering the outside world after a time when one's movement has been restricted can be exceedingly rewarding, triggering a deep appreciation of so many experiences we take for granted when well and active.

Welcome to my proverbial "Front Porch" I hope you enjoy your visit.

PART ONE

~~~

TALES OF TRAVELS
~~~

Commuting With Nature

A full moon hangs high in the pale western sky, reflecting it's blue-white aura onto the frozen landscape. To the east, the sun sends rays of rose pink over the horizon, a preview of the warm red glow, coming soon.

As I head to work on this midwinter morning, I look back at our home, nestled on a hillside sheltered by towering Norway spruce trees. I am reminded of the joys of living in this rich, still half-wild country. A light coating of snow covers the sculpted black branches of maples, the feathery green sprays of pine boughs, fields with scattered grey-brown skeletons of last year's weeds, and houses, with clouds of steam drifting from furnace flues, indications of the coziness within.

An inky black crow flaps rhythmically over a pristine white snowfield. A majestic six-point buck emerges from a thicket of shrubs, his beautiful brown coat sparkling with droplets of melted snowflakes. A blue-gray heron glides gracefully over a partially frozen stream, in search of a good fishing spot. Reassuring signs that life goes on in the cold season.

Some people seem surprised when I say that I really don't mind my twenty mile drive to work, even on most winter days. Yes the trip can get hairy when severe storms hit without warning, but by driving slowly and smoothly, I've always made it safely, only staying home during extended ice storms or blizzard conditions.

The superlative shows which stream past me each morning and evening through spring, summer, and fall more than make up for the difficult days of winter. On this chill morning I reflect that in a few short months, the sloping snowfields I am now driving past will resemble the gently rolling hills of Ireland, complete with cows and calves grazing peacefully on smooth expanses of delicate, newly green grass.

Each year I look for that magical morning, that first true day of spring, not the date on the calendar, but the real first day of the season, only known by those who are especially observant of their surroundings. The day when Mother Nature's winter bluster abruptly slows into a warm, sweet spring breeze which wafts throughout the woods and fields, fueling plants to put forth their first pale green shoots and assisting the swell of long dormant buds on trees and shrubs. The drab landscape is transformed overnight by this gentle, fleeting stage of greening. I cherish that precious phase while it lasts, knowing that soon the leaf explosion will erupt, ending the enchantment and sending spring spiraling toward summer.

But once summer is here, the ever-changing beauty of flowerbeds at the houses I pass each day enthralls me. I get a glimpse into the lives of families who stayed hidden in their warm houses over the winter. I am reminded that I consider all the people in the homes I pass on my long drive as neighbors. I think of the times when my car has broken down or I had simply pulled over to take a picture. Someone has always stopped to offer assistance. In spite of all the violence we hear of in news reports each day, at least in rural America the spirit of caring for others in time of need lives on.

Perhaps it's the space between country neighbors which draws them closer in heart.

Autumn arrives a bit more gradually than spring. Or so it seems to me. Sometimes in late July I spot a roadside tree with a spray of crimson leaves, ahead of their time. The first cicadas start then too. After that comes the first cricket chirp, then the first walnut falls from the tree; signs of summer slowly fading to fall. The forested hills sport spots of color here and there before the greatest show which comes usually in mid-October. Then the hills are ablaze with reds, oranges, and yellows, a warm patchwork quilt on display for a time before being spread upon the ground to protect tender plants from winter's wrath. The trees are bare bones once more. Another year has ended. But a new one is just around the corner.

I may not have time or energy for the walk I want to take when I reach home. But my daily car trips to and from work offer ample opportunity to keep in touch with nature; to reflect upon the serenity and beauty to be found in the changing seasons and therefore to put my own life in perspective.

The Long Way Home

We went to Home Depot to get new doorknobs.
At least that was the declared goal of the evening and we did
reach the designated destination.

But some days are meant for pleasure drives. Our homeward
journey took a spontaneously selected detour to the small town of
Jeromesville, where we enjoyed peach ice cream obtained from a
small general store. Residents strolled the streets, murals
decorated walls of buildings, and flowers bloomed from roadside
beds. Random turns down rural roads revealed spots we'd seen
years ago, and some we'd only heard stories of.

Campers and proprietors at a small lakeside campground
chatted at a picnic table as dusk descended from the open fields to
the west. Down another trail, frogs croaked and small birds
chirped evening songs aside the still waters of a nature preserve.

We arrived home, not only bearing doorknobs, but with the delight of unexpected discoveries on an idyllic August evening.

A Rural Ramble

The azure sky held just enough fluffy white clouds to spur the imagination as we watched them drift above the orchard beside the small farm-based food store.

We had gone for a drive just for fun, a thing we hadn't done for some time. The usual early August humidity was happily absent, the temperature a comfortable eighty.

Driving down the narrow farm lane, laden with the candies of our childhood, our car became a time capsule, immersed in another era. This was authentic Amish country, not at all resembling the commercial, congested tourist traps bearing that title.

Here, barefoot children padded down dirt roads or drove decked-out pony carts. In green pastures, cows and horses grazed, an increasingly rare sight these days. Sheep clustered in the shaded corner of a paddock, guarded by a large white dog who resembled them in looks, likely not in temperament.

Barn and tree swallows lined utility wires, sallying forth to sweep the air for insects, then gracefully joining their friends once more. Hawks watched for rodents from roadside crags.

We drove through open fields of rolling cropland, punctuated by tunnels of trees, large leaves fanning the warm air outside our open car windows.

Tropical orange Tiger Lilies shouted from porch-side plots while demure pink Resurrection Lilies waved on rows of airy stems. This fascinating flower is most magical, as mounded foliage appears in spring, then withers away, waiting to surprise us with it's dainty midsummer display.

Squirrels scampered across our path. Butterflies floated above bright beds of Black Eyed Susans. Crimson-cupped trumpet vines climbed rustic fence rails.

One farmyard held a fully loaded clothesline tree, something I hadn't seen in some time. Hanging clothes out to dry was a weekly ritual of summer in not so former times, when striped sheets and checked dishtowels danced in breezes behind our homes on clear, hot days. Sleep was serene on those crisp sun-scented sheets.

We meandered homeward in a happier mood on that optimal August day, souls soothed by the sweetness of summer in the country.

Sunday Drive . . . or Insights from an Aimless Auto Tour

Modern small businesses filled many of the vintage buildings that lined the Milan green.

We were surrounded by a wine store, florist, home healthcare headquarters, bar, salon and spa, two fitness facilities, and an architect's office as we ate ice cream while seated upon a classic iron park bench in front of a picture perfect bandstand/gazebo. I had never seen shrubs such as those that accented the entrance to the gazebo—apparently some sort of cedar, but with prettily frilled fronds of foliage.

Many towns we toured that day seemed shattered shells of their former selves—victims of outsourcing, income inequality, industrialized farming, and other aspects of the changing culture which has ravaged rural America.

Milan and her larger, nearby sister city, Norwalk, seemed a bit less touched by the modern day difficulties. Though not perfect by any means, they have retained many beautifully landscaped and lovingly preserved homes, and a variety of businesses, both franchises and privately owned proprietorships.

These two New England-like towns were the highlight of our day trip for me, but we also encountered many other points of interest.

Driving through open areas of cropland, we witnessed fields of corn and soybeans that stretched for miles.

One farmstead sported a unique tree which offered the impression of a dragon, with oddly outstretched branches, one of them resembling the head of the legendary fire-breathing beasts. Amish children dressed in their Sunday vest but wearing no shoes strolled roadways or stared from backseats of buggies pulled by retired racehorses.

NASA Plumbrook's tower and dome rose in the distance over cornfields near Avery. Historic tests of equipment for the space program were held there. Earlier, munitions for World War II were manufactured at the site.

We passed by Obie's, a small food and ice cream shop, formerly a tavern. The Owl Hoot, another classic bar from an earlier era of that area may be gone, destroyed during a road renovation, but Obie's remains, though in a different form.

We stopped by several cemeteries along the way, my favorite haunts these days. I love to "visit" relatives and acquaintances I've known or wish I had.

I have a favorite graveyard in a local town, more a park than a place of mourning, as dogs and owners stroll it's paths each evening.

My dad took us on Sunday dries quite often when I was a child, creeping along country lanes and telling tales of towns we passed, from former days.

How many parents do that today? So many of us speed from one point to another, never noticing the spaces between.

Summer Evening Awakening

Our drive tonight took me back in time to the days when I felt a true appreciation for nature.

It's not that the sense of oneness with the world of wildlife that resides in the woods and fields, the love for the varied shades of leaves, or the fresh scent of flowers ever left me.

It's simply that I had become obsessed with worry concerning career goals, finances, and issues of personal fulfillment. In our modern society this happens to most but I never felt it would happen to me.

I was wracked with worry in my younger days too, suffering physical symptoms of stress which I was determined to overcome.

My cure had come when I began to truly notice nature, to "find communion with her visible forms", as William Cullen Bryan would say. At the close of days spent listening to complaints of customers and dealing with the drama of co-workers I would walk on the lawn or in the woods, fill bird feeders, water flowers or simply sit outside under the vast dome of sky. In winter I would walk in snow, appreciating the sound of silence. Peace would seep into me. At least for a time I felt serene, seeing the big picture rather than wrapped up in the trivialities of human society. My inspirational material was the works of the great nature writers, my cathedral, all outdoors.

In recent times it's been more difficult to achieve this zen-like serenity, even temporarily. But as we drove that day amid seas of tall tasseled corn and lush soybeans, accented by forests, farmhouses, and fallow fields, my sense of wonder at the immense power and wisdom of nature began to return. I somehow hadn't realized that true countryside still existed. Maybe it's because I hadn't been driving the side roads, or it could be that I had simply closed my eyes to everything, in an effort to escape stress. As taking a drug to dull the senses blocks positive feelings as well as painful ones, I had put up a protective wall, just trying to get through the difficult experiences of the days without truly noticing anything at all.

We hadn't taken these types of destinationless drives for some time, but have gone on several recently. Perhaps some good will come of this stressful summer. Though country travels can't take us back to a younger time, perhaps they may lead us to what we need now.

There's No Place Like Long Sands

Dorothy followed her Yellow Brick Road, but I prefer to follow U.S. Route One north into Maine, my Oz being Long Sands, York's wondrous beach. The rock-strewn sand of this magical place stretches along the Atlantic shore opposite a row of late nineteenth to early twentieth century two story cottages. The lengthy line includes a few small shops, restaurants, and mid-century motel buildings as well as facilities for motorhomes.

I love dining at The Lobster Cove, whose chorus line of red lobster Adirondack chairs beckons beachgoers to the friendly family restaurant where they relax in front of wide rows of windows overlooking the shore. After dark, the beacon of mysterious Boone Island Lighthouse can be seen in the distance.

Perhaps the moan of a foghorn may be heard if the evening is misty.

I was first presented with the panorama of Long Sands on a sunny September morn in 2010. Leaving my lodgings in York Harbor, I headed north toward my next destination of Camden, on a mission to see most of Maine's magnificent coast. But as I entered the time warp town of York, I was loathe to drive on. I pulled into a parking space along the winding road above the sandscape, opened the door of my rental car and stepped into paradise.

The sun was warm on my shoulders, the sand shimmered. Surfers skimmed the surface of perfectly rippling waves, frothy tops forming white lacey edges above the sparkling blue water below. A man trotted a pale horse with dark mane and tail across the expanse. Young people held tight to strings of kites soaring high above the scene. Seniors scanned newspapers, leaning back in lawn chairs. Dogs frolicked in the shallows at the edge of the tide, sandpipers scurrying along beside, dodging clam shells and clumps of seaweed.

The scene was filled with activity yet felt serene. Positive energy permeated this timeless place. It seemed the spirits of early twentieth century tourists shared space with those visiting the beach that day.

When I reluctantly resumed my northward journey, I was once again amazed as I entered the downtown business district of York Beach. Not all shops were open that day, since it was off-season, but I could picture the hamlet in high summer, small stores bustling with tourists, The Goldenrod, one of the town's oldest emporiums, churning out the establishment's famous salt water taffy the same as a century ago.

In the days that followed, as I toured much of Maine's gorgeous coast, I decided visitors to the Pine Tree State would not be disappointed no matter which region they chose to explore.

My own return trips, however, have all been centered in the southern tip of the state where my favorite beach lies. I've been there in sun and storm, in several seasons, and it's always a pleasure; a peaceful adventure, filled with the wonder of nature, the camaraderie of native Mainers and would be ones like me, the sights, sounds, food, and spirit of the sea. My heart lies at Long Sands, jewel of the Yorks.

Morning has Broken

A swirl of steam rises from my coffee cup, mirroring the ethereal mist hovering above the harbor. In this magic moment all life forms pause in anticipation of first light. The moon still rules, reluctant to release her realm. But at last a kind of hush falls over the earth, just before a baby's breath breeze begins to whisper through the pine trees. Suddenly, it happens. The superstar sun shoots above the edge of the ocean to the east; a perfect beginning to that paradise that is an early autumn day in coastal Maine.

Taking a final sip of coffee, I rise from my red Adirondack chair, one of a row of multicolored examples of that most traditional furniture of downeast design. Setting my mug on the wide right armrest, I set out purposefully on the path by the water, bound for the small town beach, then the beautiful cliff path beyond.

PART TWO

~~~

NATURAL INSPIRATIONS
~~~

Reflections

at the Water's Edge

A seat at the side of a spring-fed farm pond offers an inspirational experience in any season.

On summer days a sense of oneness with the world of nature permeates the environment. Dragonflies hover above the still water, graceful swallows sweep the air, silhouetted against the cerulean blue sky, then swoop to skim the glassy green surface of the pond in their ceaseless search for insects. One can doze and dream and truly feel at ease, sheltered from the busy, modern, man-made world by nature's verdure.

Autumn brings colored leaves that sail through the air, to land and float on the wind-stirred water like so many tiny rafts. Honks of geese fill the air, their rasping music triggering thoughts of southern journeys, but the comforting chirp of crickets lulls us to stay and bask in the late-season sun.

Winter brings it's own special peace as the formerly rippling water stills into ice. An ivory blanket of snow covers all, muffling sounds to create a silence that can only be found on a cold season day. The frigid time sometimes tests our faith but this is nature's chance to rest and renew, to prepare for the rush of growth that will soon begin again.

Just as water has been the basis for life in all eras, the area around the pond seems first to stir with activity as the sun slides northward in springtime. Buds swell on overhanging trees, peepers trill from nearby wet fields, and tadpoles shimmy through the shallow water's edge. The Kingfisher's rattling call can be heard from the top of a tall tree, as a flock of northbound canvasback ducks descend, crashing the stillness, and ushering in the busy but welcome season of spring.

Twilight in the garden

A soft golden glow bathes the house and the flowers in peak bloom today. Daylilies, pointed orange petals open an hour ago are now closed, giving their energy over to the next day's blooms, still in bud. Hopefully the deer don't get to the buds before morning light signals them to open. Apparently they are a delicacy of the dainty hoofed creatures.

Bright crimson crowns of bee balm blooms rule the back of the house bed, surviving still, though a sea of weeds seeks to strangle them at their base. Too busy with work and too fragile of body and spirit this season, I seek to find solace in the garden's ability to care for itself.

Actually, the year I received the most compliments on my gardening skills was the summer my mother suffered illness which culminated in her death in September. I don't know what that says about my gardening skills, but I am sure Mother Nature knows more about nurturing a lush display than I do. The plants may not be the chosen ones but apparently it doesn't matter.

The beautiful golden light is now disappearing, replaced by a dim blue aura. Early fireflies flash faintly across the sea of tall grass on the other side of the road.

Sitting here in the backyard, I always feel like a queen overseeing her realm. The height from the road makes the vehicles appear as part of another world, though the noise does invade my territory.

Today's strong breeze has now stilled, the trees unmoving. I won't need to water, as the four o'clock brief but strong thundershower refreshed everything with one fourth inch of rain, and the nourishing nitrogen provided by strong lightning

Nature's Celebration

Who doesn't have fond memories of fireworks? The light and sound shows held along with the Fourth of July holiday never fail to take me back to childhood. Often keeping our fingers crossed that the threat of thundershowers would not materialize, my father, mother and I would drive into town and park in a lot along with many other rural residents of the county. We would ooh and ahh at the sparkling displays, my favorite being the ones that screeched after exploding, sounding a bit like squeaky chalk scraping the sky all the way to the ground.

But if I don't make it to see a fireworks display this year, that's okay too. Seated in the sun in my lawn chair this afternoon, it's as if I'm watching nature's own Independence Day celebration. Bright crimson bee balm blooms are ablaze in the sun, spiky upturned petals reminiscent of popping firecrackers. Below them, pots of petunias, red petals glowing in the luminous light accent the show. Deep blue is provided by sprays of frilly lobelia. Huge white balls of geraniums, along with small star shaped impatiens provide detail.

Dappling sunlight and gentle breezes sway the flowers to and fro. Suddenly, a cloud of hummingbirds descends on the scene, seeming like a grand finale. The entire performance is set against the backdrop of a brilliant blue sky, white clouds drifting dreamily over all.

However one celebrates the fourth, the month of July provides a backdrop of drama. Arguably the most active month of the year, nature's peak energy flow spurs the growth and maturity of corn in the fields, tomatoes and zucchini in the garden, and all of nature's greenery. Yet amid all this activity, quiet moments may be found. An hour stolen for reading a favorite book in the deep shade of a maple; an evening spent on a porch swing watching fireflies emerge from dew damp grass.

Girlhood Memories and Graceful Geraniums

Sometimes memories are triggered in most odd ways. This morning, while enjoying coffee on the porch, I took note of a bright red bloom on an ivy geranium, a particularly long-stemmed one which seemed to be reaching out of it's hanging basket to demand my attention.

Immediately I could see my mother, readying herself for church blotting the bright crimson lipstick she wore every time she went into town. Vividly red lips were as expected as high-heeled shoes in mid-twentieth century America.

I don't miss the days when formal attire was required even for housework (if one believes the behavior of June Cleaver to be an accurate portrayal of a nineteen fifties housewife). But I do love geraniums, as a symbol of classic style. Some friends feel they're too common to be attractive, with all the new bedding plants available today. But their beauty is timeless, their presence on my porch from mid-May often until well into October each year a reassuring symbol of the sweetness of summer, and this morning serving as messenger from the spirit of my mother.

Midsummer Eve Dream

On my back in the dew damp grass, my mind is light years away, lost in the diamond dusted velvet blanket which is the summer night sky. I mine the memories of childhood for the names of the constellations.

The names and the myths behind them take me far back in time. Sitting up, I see the sky reflected in front of me. A myriad of fireflies, natures nighttime jewels, flash in formation. Their tiny bright lights create ever changing constellations above the darkened meadow before me; heaven on earth.

Mother Maple

My friend has a tree she calls Mother Cedar.

We both feel a connection to cultures which regard nature's varied forms with honor and respect. Nature is, after all, the manifestation of a higher power, and our source for sustenance of body and soul.

Trees, by species, carry certain traits, and, as with all creatures and creations, each individual of each species has a personality of it's own, sensed by those in tune with subtleties.

Behind my house, at the end of a trail to an open field framed by forest, reigns the Queen of Silver Maples. The most magnificent one I've seen.

Her trunk's girth must be nearly four feet across. The many-leaved branches of her crown stretch far into the sky, covered by a cap of delicate, silver-lined leaves.

Gazing up into her canopy, I feel her strength, as she absorbs energy from both earth and sun. The black and gray patterned bark, grizzled with age , some branches covered with lichen, exudes life-force energy nonetheless. She is an inspiration to me as I age. A reminder of the value of wisdom, strength, and courage that comes from seeing many cycles of seasons pass.

Evening by the Copse

Standing at the edge of the yard I stare into another world. The slanting rays of the late day sun send muted light into the clearing just to the west of the mown lawn line.

Fluffy boughs of white pine reach out from the south, arching branches of hickory wave wands of large palmed leaves from the north.

The area between is an enchanted world, accented by tall New York Ironweed, tops gracefully capped with purple crowns. Drooping Goldenrod sprays provide balance with gray-gold impressionistically blurred clusters of tiny florets.

I suddenly see the Tulip Tree I thought had died managed to survive and flourish. Trunk severed by a fallen wild cherry limb several seasons ago, it's now nearly ten feet tall with well-shaped limbs grown all around.

Trees teach many things. I noticed this Tulip Poplar's rebirth on an eve when I'm in need of a strong symbol of the rewards of resilience.

The Ultimate Plein-Air Painter

A cool, breezy, sun-dappled day. The hillside across the way is a museum quality painting.

Solar rays play across the mounded tops of trees, each a unique species of particular age, shape, and condition. Some covered in glossy dark leaves, some a pale delicate spring-like green, some with a tinge of yellow, yet they seem one complete entity; a sea of green, rippled by wind and the changing light patterns as clouds with flat dark bottoms and tall white tops like large sails, cross the sun then move off again.

They're not clouds that race ahead of storms, but rather the type that follow cool fronts. This front was a welcome arrival after a series of sultry days.

Soft feathery spruce branches drape across the right foreground of the masterpiece, while large, artfully shaped shiny leaves of hickory wave gracefully on slender stems, a contrast to the coarse craggy bark of the the tall strong trunk. Lining the lower edge, are hosta, sporting heart shaped leaves of green piped with white, as

*well as the large, showy Thunderbolt variety, with vividly ribbed
leaves splashed with chartreuse accents.*

*The challenge of the Plein-air painter is to capture such views,
not simply the beauty we see with our eyes, but to impart the feel
of air and sun on skin, the lightness that fills one's soul when
sitting outside, truly experiencing an expansive scene.*

*Those of us who realize that the loftiness of that goal exceeds
our practical talents simply strive to store the peace of such places
in our souls, pulling them up in our minds on difficult days*

Leaf Labyrinth

Looking up from my lounge chair where I repose amid the Eden of an August afternoon, I find myself enamored by the artistry of foliage which shades me from the seasonally shimmering sun.

Branches of varied trees crisscross gracefully above me; delicate fronds of dogwood, large palmate-leaved hickory, small pinnate patterned walnut, prettily shaped maple, attractively topped by fine-needled spruce, extend out from their trunks in alternating layers.

Randomly unplanned, yet the arrangement seems perfect, just as this day has turned out to be.

Light at the End of the Summer

*Spotted Touch-me-not blooms glow from the forested field like
orange-red gemstones, quivering on leafy stems, thus the plant is
often referred to as Jewelweed.*

*I recently heard it's an invasive species but I enjoy it's beauty
just the same.*

*The drought of August has muted the growth of the impatiens
but the surviving stems sport bright red and white stars, shining
through the tufts of crab grass surrounding them.*

*Silvery leaves of the sage plant and pine-like fronds of rosemary
aren't prolific but still they waft their stimulating scents into the
moist summer air.*

*I couldn't care for my plants much of the summer, but some of
them toughed it out, surprising me with a few cheerful blossoms,
which I appreciate much more than the bounties of blooms I took
for granted in summers when I was strong, healthy, and able to
weed and water.*

*Like me, they've made it through a trying time and are doing
their best to recover, contributing what they can as they are able.*

Thank you for selecting Volume I of Front Porch Perspectives. Future versions are planned as well as fiction and non-fiction publications pertaining to vintage items and culture, local history, and cozy mystery.

For updates and entertaining posts, please follow:

Penny Mason Publications on Facebook
thepennymasonpost.wordpress.com
Contact: pennymasonpublications@gmail.com

Sincerely,
Kathryn Gerwig